D0876416

Energy in Motion

By Melissa Stewart

Subject Consultant
Andrew Fraknoi
Chair, Astronomy Program
Foothill College
Los Altos Hills, California

Reading Consultant
Cecilia Minden-Cupp, PhD
Former Director of the Language and Literacy Program
Harvard Graduate School of Education
Cambridge, Massachusetts

Children's Press®
A Division of Scholastic Inc.
New York   Toronto   London   Auckland   Sydney
Mexico City   New Delhi   Hong Kong
Danbury, Connecticut

Special thanks to my favorite physicist, Gerard Fairley,
for his help in preparing this manuscript

Designer: Herman Adler Design
Photo Researcher: Caroline Anderson
The photo on the cover shows girls playing soccer.

Library of Congress Cataloging-in-Publication Data

Stewart, Melissa.
  Energy in motion / by Melissa Stewart; consultants, Andrew Fraknoi,
Cecilia Minden-Cupp.
      p. cm. — (Rookie Read-About Science)
  Includes index.
  ISBN 0-516-24956-8 (lib. bdg.)   0-516-23736-5 (pbk.)
  1. Motion—Juvenile literature. 2. Force and energy—Juvenile literature.
I. Title. II. Series.
    QC133.5.S738 2006
    531'.6—dc22
                                                        2005021754

CHILDREN'S PRESS, and ROOKIE READ-ABOUT®,
and associated logos are trademarks and/or registered trademarks
of Scholastic Library Publishing. SCHOLASTIC and associated logos
are trademarks and/or registered trademarks of Scholastic Inc.

1 2 3 4 5 6 7 8 9 10 R 15 14 13 12 11 10 09 08 07 06

When you run, you have motion. You move from one end of the soccer field to the other.

When you do a somersault, you have motion. You move across a mat.

When you swing, you have motion. You move up and down. The swing has motion, too.

A swing cannot move by itself.

But hop on and pump
your legs. Then you get
a fun ride!

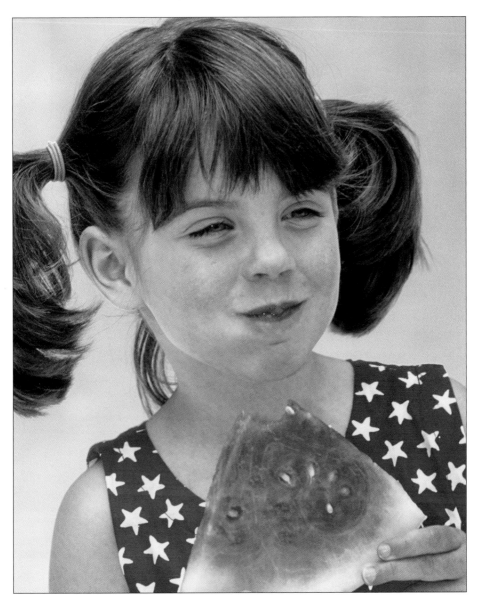

The muscles in your legs make the swing move. Your muscles need a lot of energy to move the swing.

Where do muscles get their energy? From the food you eat.

When a swing is moving, it has energy, too.

The faster you pump your legs, the higher you will go. The faster the swing goes, the more energy it has.

13

When you jump off the
swing, it starts to slow down.

Now the swing has
less energy.

If your dad pushes you on the swing, you get a free ride. Your leg muscles don't have to do any work. Your dad's arm muscles do the work.

Now let the rubber band go.
The stored-up energy changes
to energy in motion.

The rubber band zips
across the room.

Now get two tennis balls.

Lift one high above your head. Hold the other one near your waist. Drop both balls.

What happens?

25

When you drop the balls, the stored-up energy changes to energy in motion.

The ball you lifted above your head will bounce higher. It had more stored-up energy.

Look around your house and yard.

Can you think of some other ways to observe energy in motion?

29

Words You Know

motion

muscles

rubber band

soccer

somersault

swing

tennis balls

31

Index

About the Author

Award-winning author Melissa Stewart has always been fascinated with the natural world and enjoys sharing it with others. She has written more than sixty science books for children.

Photo Credits

Photographs © 2006: PhotoEdit: 6, 30 top left (Kayte M. Deioma), cover, 10, 13 (David Young-Wolff); Superstock, Inc./age fotostock: 3, 31 top left; all other photographs copyright © 2006 Christine Osinski.